Chris CAROLS

Illustrations by Margaret Tempest

CARNIVAL

JOY TO THE WORLD

Joy to the world! The Lord is come.
Let Earth receive her King.
Let ev'ry heart prepare him room,
And Heav'n and Nature sing,
And Heav'n and Nature sing,
And Heav'n, and Heav'n and Nature sing.

Joy to the world! The Saviour reigns.
Let men their songs employ,
While fields and floods, rocks, hills, and plains
Repeat the sounding joy,
Repeat the sounding joy,
Repeat, repeat the sounding joy.

He rules the world with truth and grace
And makes the nations prove
The glories of His righteousness
And wonders of His love,
And wonders of His love,
And wonders, wonders of His love.

OH COME, ALL YE FAITHFUL

Oh come, all ye faithful,
Joyful and triumphant,
Oh come ye, oh come ye to Bethlehem.
Come and behold Him, born the King
   of Angels.

CHORUS:
Oh come, let us adore Him,
Oh come, let us adore Him,
Oh come, let us adore Him,
Christ the Lord!

Sing, choirs of angels,
Sing in exultation.
Sing, all ye citizens of Heav'n, above:
"Glory to God, in the highest."

CHORUS:
Oh come, let us adore Him,
Oh come, let us adore Him,
Oh come, let us adore Him,
Christ the Lord!

Yea, Lord, we greet Thee,
Born this happy morning.
Jesu, to Thee be glory giv'n,
Word of the Father, now in flesh
   appearing.

CHORUS:
Oh come, let us adore Him,
Oh come, let us adore Him,
Oh come, let us adore Him,
Christ the Lord!

AWAY IN A MANGER

Away in a manger, no crib for a bed,
The little Lord Jesus lay down His sweet head.
The stars in the bright sky looked down where
    He lay:
The little Lord Jesus, asleep in the hay.

The cattle are lowing. The baby awakes,
But little Lord Jesus, no crying He makes.
I love Thee, Lord Jesus! Look down from
    the sky,
And stay by my side until morning is nigh.

Be near me, Lord Jesus! I ask Thee to stay
Close by me forever and love me, I pray.
Bless all the dear children in Thy tender care,
And fit us for heaven to live with Thee there.

GOOD KING WENCESLAS

Good King Wenceslas looked out
On the Feast of Stephen,
When the snow lay 'round about.
Deep and crisp and even.
Brightly shone the moon that night,
Though the frost was cruel,
When a poor man came in sight,
Gath'ring winter fuel.

"Hither, page, and stand by me!
If thou knowst it telling,
Yonder peasant – who is he?
Where and what his dwelling?"
"Sire, he lives a good league hence,
Underneath the mountain,
Right against the forest fence
By Saint Agnes' Fountain."

"Bring me flesh and bring me wine!
Bring me pine-logs hither!
Thou and I will see him dine
When we bear them thither."
Page and monarch, forth they went;
Forth they went together,
Through the rude wind's wild lament
And the bitter weather.

"Sire, the night grows darker now,
And the wind blows stronger.
Fails my heart – I know not how
I can go no longer!"
"Mark my footsteps my good page.
Tread thou in them boldly.
Thou shall feel this winter's rage
Freeze thy blood less coldly."

In his master's steps he trod,
Where the snow lay dinted.
Heat was in the very sod
Which the Saint had printed.
Therefore, Christian men, be sure,
Wealth or rank possessing,
Ye who now will bless the poor
Shall yourselves find blessing.

IT CAME UPON
THE MIDNIGHT CLEAR

It came upon the midnight clear,
That glorious song of old,
From angels bending near the Earth
To touch their harps of gold:
"Peace on the Earth! Good will to men,
From Heaven's all-gracious King!"
The world in solemn stillness lay
To hear the angels sing.

But with the woes of sin and strife,
The world has suffered long.
Beneath the angels-strain have rolled
Two thousand years of wrong;
And man, at war with man, hears not
The love-song which they bring.
Oh, hush the noise, ye men of strife,
And hear the angels sing!

For lo! The days are hast'ning on,
By prophet-bards foretold,
When, with the ever-circling years,
Comes round the age of gold;
When peace shall over all the earth
Its ancient splendours fling,
And the whole world give back the song
Which now the angels sing.

WE THREE KINGS OF ORIENT ARE

We three kings of Orient are.
Bearing gifts, we traverse afar –
Field and fountain, moor and mountain –
Following yonder star.

CHORUS:
Oh, star of wonder, star of night,
Star of royal beauty bright,
Westward leading, still proceeding,
Guide us to thy perfect light.

(MELCHIOR)
Born a king on Bethlehem plain –
Gold I bring, to crown Him again –
King for ever, ceasing never,
Over us all to reign.

CHORUS:
Oh, star of wonder, star of night,
Star of royal beauty bright,
Westward leading, still proceeding,
Guide us to thy perfect light.

(GASPAR)
Frankincense to offer have I.
Incense owns a Deity nigh.
Prayer and praising, all men raising,
Worship Him, God most high!

CHORUS:
Oh, star of wonder, star of night,
Star of royal beauty bright,
Westward leading, still proceeding,
Guide us to thy perfect light.

(BALTHAZAR)
Myrrh is mine, its bitter perfume
Breathes a life of gathering gloom,
Sorrowing, sighing, bleeding, dying,
Sealed in a stone-cold tomb.

CHORUS:
Oh, star of wonder, star of night,
Star of royal beauty bright,
Westward leading, still proceeding,
Guide us to thy perfect light.

(ALL)
Glorious now, behold Him arise:
King and God and sacrifice!
Heav'n sings, Hallelujah, Hallelujah,
Earth to the Heav'ns replies.

CHORUS:
Oh, star of wonder, star of night,
Star of royal beauty bright,
Westward leading, still proceeding,
Guide us to thy perfect light.

OH LITTLE TOWN OF BETHLEHEM

Oh little town of Bethlehem,
How still we see thee lie!
Above thy deep and dreamless sleep
The silent stars go by.
Yet in thy dark streets shineth
The everlasting light:
The hopes and fears of all the years
Are met in thee tonight.

How silently, how silently,
The wondrous gift is giv'n!
So God imparts to human hearts
The blessings of His Heav'n.
No ear may hear His coming,
But in this world of sin,
Where meek souls will receive Him, still
The dear Christ enters in.

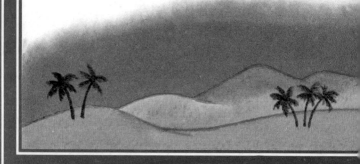

Oh holy Child of Bethlehem,
Descend to us, we pray.
Cast out our sin and enter in.
Be born in us today!
We hear the Christmas angels
Their great glad tidings tell.
Oh, come to us, abide with us,
Our Lord Emmanuel.

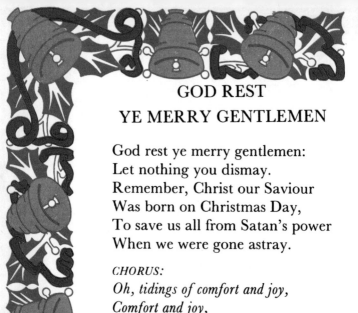

GOD REST
YE MERRY GENTLEMEN

God rest ye merry gentlemen:
Let nothing you dismay.
Remember, Christ our Saviour
Was born on Christmas Day,
To save us all from Satan's power
When we were gone astray.

CHORUS:
Oh, tidings of comfort and joy,
Comfort and joy,
Oh, tidings of comfort and joy!

From God our Heav'nly Father
A blessed angel came
And unto certain shepherds
Brought tidings of the same:
How that in Bethlehem was born
The son of God by name.

CHORUS:
Oh, tidings of comfort and joy,
Comfort and joy,
Oh, tidings of comfort and joy!

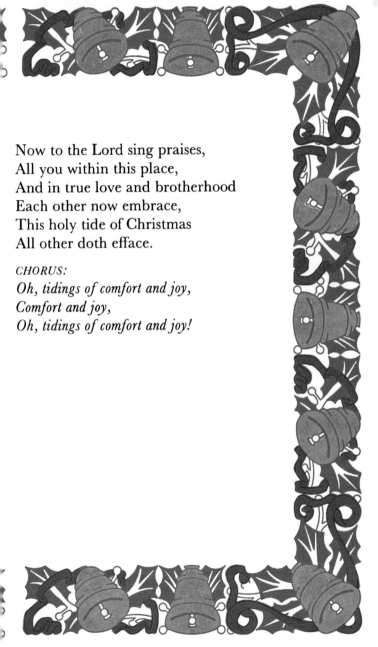

Now to the Lord sing praises,
All you within this place,
And in true love and brotherhood
Each other now embrace,
This holy tide of Christmas
All other doth efface.

CHORUS:
Oh, tidings of comfort and joy,
Comfort and joy,
Oh, tidings of comfort and joy!

HARK! THE HERALD ANGELS SING

Hark! The herald angels sing,
"Glory to the newborn King!
Peace on Earth and mercy mild,
God and sinners reconciled"
Joyful all ye nations, rise!
Join the triumph of the skies,
With th'angelic host, proclaim,
"Christ is born in Bethlehem!"

CHORUS:
Hark! The herald angels sing,
"Glory to the newborn King!"

Christ, by highest Heav'n adored;
Christ, the everlasting Lord:
Late in time, behold Him come,
Offspring of the Virgin's womb.
Veiled in flesh the Godhead see.
Hail th'Incarnate Deity
Pleased as Man with men to dwell –
Jesus, our Emmanuel!

CHORUS:
Hark! The herald angels sing,
"Glory to the newborn King!"

Hail, the Heav'n born Prince of Peace!
Hail, the Sun of Righteousness!
Light and life to all He brings,
Ris'n with healing in His wings.
Mild He lays His glory by,
Born that man no more may die,
Born to raise the sons of earth,
Born to give them second birth.

CHORUS:
Hark! The herald angels sing,
"Glory to the newborn King!"

WHAT CHILD IS THIS?

What child is this who, laid to rest,
On Mary's lap is sleeping;
Whom angels greet with anthems sweet,
While shepherds watch are keeping?

CHORUS:
This, this is Christ the King,
Whom shepherds guard and angels sing.
Haste, haste to bring Him laud,
The Babe, the Son of Mary.

Why lies He in such mean estate,
Where ox and ass are feeding?
Good Christian, fear for sinners here,
The silent Word is pleading.

CHORUS:
This, this is Christ the King,
Whom shepherds guard and angels sing.
Haste, haste to bring Him laud,
The Babe, the Son of Mary.

So bring Him incense, gold and myrrh.
Come, peasants, kings, to own Him.
The King of Kings salvation brings –
Let loving hearts enthrone Him!

CHORUS:
This, this is Christ the King,
Whom shepherds guard and angels sing.
Haste, haste to bring Him laud,
The Babe, the Son of Mary.

ONCE IN ROYAL DAVID'S CITY

Once in Royal David's City
Stood a lowly cattle shed,
Where a mother laid her baby
In a manger for His bed;
Mary was that mother mild,
Jesus Christ her little child.

He came down to earth from Heaven
Who is God and Lord of all,
And His shelter was a stable,
And His cradle was a stall;
With the poor and mean and lowly,
Lived on earth our Saviour holy.

And, through all His wondrous childhood
He would honour and obey,
Love and watch the lowly mother,
In whose gentle arms He lay;
Christian children all must be
Mild, obedient, good as He.

For He is our childhood's pattern,
Day by day like us He grew.
He was little, weak and helpless,
Tears and smile like us He knew;
And He feeleth for our sadness,
And He shareth in our gladness.

And our eyes at last shall see Him,
Thro' His own redeeming love,
For that child so dear and gentle
Is our Lord in heav'n above;
And He leads His children on
To the place where He is gone.

THE FIRST NOEL

The first Noel the angels did say
Was to certain poor shepherds in fields as
   they lay –
In fields where they lay, keeping their sheep,
On a cold winter's night that was so deep.

CHORUS:
Noel, Noel, Noel, Noel,
Born is the King of Israel!

They looked up and saw a star,
Shining in the East, beyond them far.
And to the Earth it gave great light,
And so it continued, both day and night.

CHORUS:
Noel, Noel, Noel, Noel,
Born is the King of Israel!

And by the light of that same star
Three Wise Men came from country far.
To seek for a King was their intent,
And to follow the star wherever it went.

CHORUS:
Noel, Noel, Noel, Noel,
Born is the King of Israel!

This star drew nigh to the northwest.
O'er Bethlehem it took its rest,
And there it did both stop and stay
Right over the place where Jesus lay.

CHORUS:
Noel, Noel, Noel, Noel,
Born is the King of Israel!

Then entered in those Wise Men three,
Fell reverently upon their knee,
And offered there, in His presence,
Their gold and myrrh and frankincense.

CHORUS:
Noel, Noel, Noel, Noel,
Born is the King of Israel!

Then let us all, with one accord,
Sing praises to our Heavenly Lord,
That hath made Heav'n and earth of naught.
And with his blood mankind hath bought.

CHORUS:
Noel, Noel, Noel, Noel,
Born is the King of Israel!

SILENT NIGHT

Silent night, holy night!
All is calm, all is bright
'Round yon Virgin Mother and Child –
Holy infant, so tender and mild.
Sleep in heavenly peace,
Sleep in heavenly peace.

Silent night, holy night!
Shepherds first saw the sight.
Glories stream from Heaven afar,
Heav'nly hosts sing "Alleluia,
Christ the Saviour is born,
Christ the Saviour is born!"

Silent night, holy night!
Son of God, love's pure light,
Radiance beams from Thy holy face,
With the dawn of redeeming grace.
Jesus, Lord at Thy birth,
Jesus, Lord at Thy birth!

ANGELS WE HAVE HEARD ON HIGH

Angels we have heard on high,
Sweetly singing o'er the plains;
And the mountains, in reply,
Echoing their joyful strains:

CHORUS:
Gloria in excelsis Deo,
Gloria in excelsis Deo!

Shepherds, why this jubilee?
Why your joyful strains prolong?
What the gladsome tidings be
That inspire your heav'nly song?

CHORUS:
Gloria in excelsis Deo,
Gloria in excelsis Deo!

DECK THE HALLS

Deck the halls with boughs of holly.
Fa la la la la, la la la la.
'Tis the season to be jolly.
Fa la la la la, la la la la.
Don we now our gay apparel.
Fa la la la la, la la la la.
Troll the ancient Yuletide carol.
Fa la la la la, la la la la.

See the blazing Yule before us.
Fa la la la la, la la la la.
Strike the harp and join the chorus.
Fa la la la la, la la la la.
Follow me in merry measure –
Fa la la la la, la la la la.
While I tell of Yuletide treasure.
Fa la la la la, la la la la.

Fast away the old year passes.
Fa la la la la, la la la la.
Hail the new, ye lads and lasses
Fa la la la la, la la la la.
Sing we joyous, all together –
Fa la la la la, la la la la.
Heedless of the wind and weather.
Fa la la la la, la la la la.

Carnival
An imprint of the Children's Division
of the Collins Publishing Group
8 Grafton Street, London W1X 3LA

Published by Carnival 1988.

ISBN 0 00 194548 3

Printed and bound in Great Britain by
PURNELL BOOK PRODUCTION   LIMITED
A MEMBER OF BPCC plc